Anteaters to Zebras

Alan Fletcher

THIS BOOK BELONGS TO

_____

WRITE YOUR NAME IN CAPITAL LETTERS

this book belongs to

_____

write your name in small letters

ANTEATER
anteater

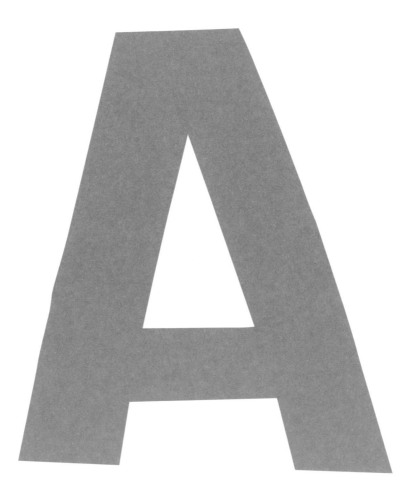

BEAR
bear

CAT
cat

DOG
dog

ELEPHANT
elephant

FROG
frog

GIRAFFE
giraffe

IGUANA
iguana

JACKASS
jackass

KANGAROO
kangaroo

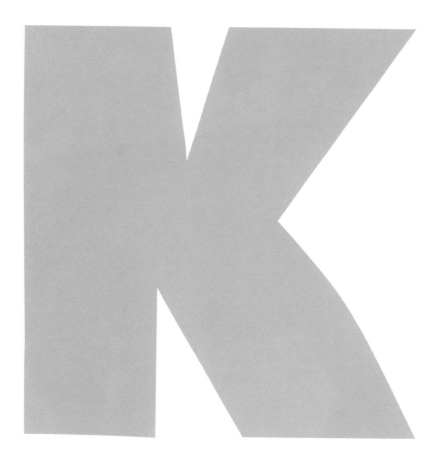

LION
lion

MONKEY
monkey

NANNY GOAT
nanny goat

OCTOPUS
octopus

PIG
pig

QUEEN BEE
queen bee

RABBIT
rabbit

SQUIRREL
squirrel

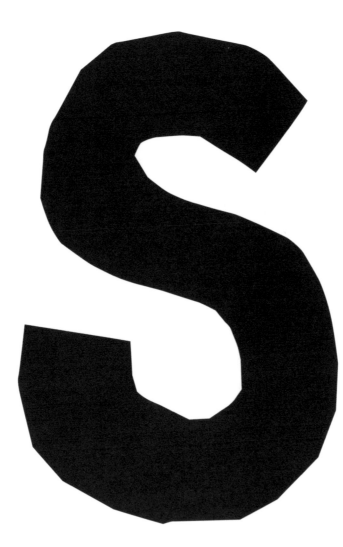

TORTOISE
tortoise

UNICORN
unicorn

VULTURE
vulture

WHALE
whale

X-RAY FISH
x-ray fish

YETI
yeti

ZEBRA
zebra

First published 2011 by order of the Tate Trustees
by Tate Publishing, a division of Tate Enterprises Ltd,
Millbank, London SW1P 4RG
www.tate.org.uk/publishing

A catalogue record for this book is available from the British Library

ISBN 978 1 84976 004 1

Distributed in the United States and Canada by ABRAMS, New York

Library of Congress Control Number: 2011940636

Designed by Alan Fletcher
Dedicated to his grandson Tobia Fletcher
Brought to life by Raffaella Fletcher and Daniel Chehade
Technics by Roger Taylor
Printed in Spain by Grafos SA
Printed on FSC and PEFC certified paper

MIX
From responsible
sources
FSC
www.fsc.org   FSC® C012329